2001: A POETRY ODYSSEY
WIRRAL

Edited by Sarah Andrew

First published in Great Britain in 2001 by
YOUNG WRITERS
Remus House,
Coltsfoot Drive,
Peterborough, PE2 9JX
Telephone (01733) 890066

HB ISBN 0 75432 422 2
SB ISBN 0 75432 423 0

FOREWORD

Young Writers was established in 1991 with the aim to promote creative writing in children, to make reading and writing poetry fun.

This year the 2001: A Poetry Odyssey competition again proved to be a tremendous success with over 50,000 entries received nationwide.

The amount of hard work and effort put into each entry impressed us all, and is reflective of the teaching skills in schools today.

The task of selecting poems for publication was a difficult one but nevertheless, an enjoyable experience. We hope you are as pleased with the final selection in *2001: A Poetry Odyssey Wirral* as we are.

To Nana

A present for Mothers day, March 2001.

My poem is on page 102.

Lots of love from Hannah.

HBradon

CONTENTS

Jessica Potts	70
Terry Orange	71
Vicki Campbell	72
Nicola Fielding	73
Cassandra McMahon	74
Carl Lewis	75
Ben Gouldson	76
Vanessa Johnstone	77
Chris Wall	78
Suzanne Jackson	79

West Kirby Grammar School For Girls

Hannah Langford Spencer	80
Christine Elizabeth Lemon	81
Lisa Jones	82
Gemma Wright	84
Jayne Macdonald	85
Charlotte Houghton	86
Stephanie Noble	87
Rachael Cleator	88
Emma Fielding	89
Jenn Cleave	90
Philippa Hirst	91
Charlotte Hugman	92
Sarah Coral Richards	93
Jennifer Evans	94
Hayley Fairclough	95
Sarah Flaherty	96
Vikki Johnston	98
Julia Morris	99
Rebecca Ryan	100
Libbie Sprigge	101
Hannah Bradon	102
Dorcas Riley	103
Jennifer Harney	104
Jessica Bennett	105
Justine McLaughlin	106
Helen Louise Wildman	107

The Poems

THE CITY

The city, the city is ever so busy.
The cars, cars are ever so fast.
They pollute the air like passing wind
in a small room.
The buildings, the buildings are so tall,
It feels like they are falling down on you.

Sammy Scott (13)
Bebington High School

DOTTY, DOTTY, WHERE CAN YOU BE?

Dotty, Dotty, where can you be?
You're not in the cupboard,
You're not under the stairs,
So where are you Dotty?
You cannot be outside.
Or are you outside?
I thought not, it is too cold outside.
So where are you Dotty?
I hear some creaking, she must be upstairs,
I'm coming upstairs Dotty.
Are you in my room Dotty?
Oh, there you are Dotty,
You're in the spare room.

Linzi Dobson (14)
Bebington High School

WALKING TO SCHOOL

I was walking to school on a cold and wet day
Wind howling all around me
I heard a rumbling in the clouds
Suddenly the wind picks up
Blowing everything about
Then the rain started
Sitting in the classroom
So cold and scared.

Claire Williams (14)
Bebington High School

THE BOXER

The noise is shocking
The ring is rocking
As I step through the ropes
The cheers grow higher
My nerves are going faster
My pulse is racing
The bell rings, I can imagine Hell
The big boxer comes over
Punch! I am seeing stars
I hit the deck
      Everyone is screaming
      Get up!
      Get up!
The fight is over
My lights are out.
      7, 8, 9, 10 - *You're out!*

David Clampitt (13)
Bebington High School

ARE YOU RIDING?

Flip, skip, overload
How much, I asked, is it to ride?
Free at first, I remember those words
They're the words that will remain.

Pop, sniff, make a spliff
Addiction hard, I do admit
To jump on board is very easy
But not as simple to get off believe me.

If you choose to join the crew
Just remember what's best for you
Empty pockets, no control, death threats
Sickness, do you enrol?

If you're feeling down, this ain't the answer
If you're a rider, the doctors won't 'ave yer.
You'll be alone, alone in this never-ending hole
If you never took that offer, you'd have been better on the whole.

Before you board, just remember
You are all you've got.

Is it your choice to ride it?
Or had you better *not.*

Rosie Wright (14)
Bebington High School

ALIEN LANDING

The spaceship hovered above the shops and houses,
It came from far away,
From the corner of the solar system,
And now it was here on Earth.
It was big and scary,
With bright colours and flashing lights,
It landed with a loud roar like a lion.
It let off steams and gases,
That made the sky look foggy,
There was a putrid smell that came from the ship,
And as soon as it reached my nostrils my eyes began to water.
The atmosphere was freezing cold,
There was then a rippling heat,
The door cracked open . . .
Stood there was an alien!
Long and thin,
Piercing eyes,
Green and grey with flashing colours.

Mark Courtney (12)
Bebington High School

ALIEN POEM

The alien spaceship landed in our playground,
It made a loud whirling wind sound,
The whole school was staggered to see,
An alien emerging startled as can be.

Everyone was stunned with mouths open wide,
To see another hideous alien appearing inside.
Were they going to kill us? Nobody knew.
What should we do? The alien just came out of the blue.

It was horrific and green,
And looked rather mean.
It had a big, staring eye like a round pie,
Which was in the middle of its belly
And a nose on its head that was slimy like jelly.

Mr Burns, the headteacher, ran into school,
To ring the Ghostbusters and see if they would know what to do.
They came to our school and said 'We only kill ghosts.'
The situation was frightening.
We could be flattened like toast!
They said 'We'll have a go but we really don't know.'
But before they could try, the aliens had flown high.
Off they went in their spaceship, up in the sky.
They went without a word, not even a goodbye!

Samantha Jones (12)
Bebington High School

ALIEN POEM

Aliens are here!
The spaceship lands with a crash.
A ramp lowers down
And hits the ground with a bash.

The alien emerged from the ship.
It looked ugly and mean.
One big eyeball on the stomach,
Its skin was lumpy and green.

The alien walked towards me.
It crawled instead of walked,
Because the alien had four legs.
Then it began to talk.

'Noy the hu nu hep ta lo courd
La me ef a cu le mere!'
I don't like the look of this,
I'm getting out of here!

Glen Cooper (12)
Bebington High School

THE ALIENS' DAY OUT

The aliens from outer space,
Came down to take over the human race.
All the aliens green and blue,
Arrived in their ship,
Which was shaped like a shoe.
The blue and green aliens left their ship,
They went to the beach and,
They went to the dock,
They even bought ice-cream from the ice-cream shop.
When they got bored they went to the zoo,
They saw elephants, giraffes,
And the monkeys too.
The aliens heard music,
Which brought them to stare,
At the disco on Dilnot Street,
They had to go there.
So they went to the party,
They started to dance,
They ate all of the food,
So the party ended early.
The aliens went back to their ship,
And told the others about their trip.

Julia Reid (12)
Bebington High School

MY ALIEN POEM

This spaceship came from out of the sky,
It was all silvery-blue.
Everyone thought they were going to die,
Will they kill us? Nobody knew.

Should I go out and see what they are like,
Or should I just leave them alone?
The alien came out and gave me a fright,
He looked like he was all on his own.

Really, inside he was friendly and nice,
He loved to play with the children.
He had very good manners and was very polite,
He was really one in a million.

His skin was all green and slimy,
His four eyes were suspended on stalks.
He came and stood right beside me,
Just look at the way that he walks.

All week we played, laughed and walked,
He became a really good friend.
We learnt to swim, dance and talk,
We wished it would never end.

Time does fly,
And he had to go home.
So we said our goodbyes
And said we would phone.

These alien exchanges are really great,
I gave the alien my photo.
Next year, I really can't wait
To visit his planet Pluto.

Christine Mulheirn (12)
Bebington High School

ALIEN ALERT!

A liens are here!
L anding in the school car park.
I cy-cold feeling up my spine.
E ating everything in sight.
N othing left to see.
S o they go back to their planet.

Emily Thomas (13)
Bebington High School

ALIENS

They're coming . . .
Coming from outer space
Coming to meet the human race.

They've landed . . .
Landed in the park
In the middle of the night
It's very dark.

Something's emerging . . .
It's slimy and green
I can't bear looking at it
It's the ugliest thing I've ever seen!

Sean McKinnon (12)
Bebington High School

ALIEN POEM

The aliens came from nowhere,
Flashing lights and loud sirens.
Then suddenly the clouds went black,
As the spaceship landed.

All I could see was mist and fog,
The wind was as powerful as a twister.
Then the spaceship emerged,
Out of all the mist and fog.
It was amazing as everyone stood
Still looking startled.

At first I couldn't believe my eyes,
That a spaceship had actually landed
On the school playground.

It went quiet,
As the door of the ship opened.
Everyone took a step back.
The door opened like a child
Taking off the lid of sweets
But in slow motion.

The aliens came out, *gunge* too!
They were horrible!
They were hideous!
They were revolting!
But most of all they were after us!

Stephanie Bretherton (12)
Bebington High School

FRANK'S DOG

My dog is white like snow,
It runs fast like a cheetah,
It wags its tail when it is happy
I love my dog Rosie.

Frank Crisp (15)
Foxfield School

NEW CAR

We've got a new car,
A silver Renault Scenic.
It has lots of space
And a new bonnet,
Central locking
And the doors unlock like magic.
I sit in the back,
Listening to tapes
And looking out.

Andrew Lewis (15)
Foxfield School

MY MUM

My mum is:
Very kind,
Getting me ready in the morning,
Drink and biscuits after school,
Tidying up the house,
Hoovering,
A bedtime story.

Laura Reidy (14)
Foxfield School

MY SWING

My swing is green like grass,
It goes up in the sky like a bird.
It is in the garden with the trees,
I have lots of fun on my swing.

Christopher Edwards (14)
Foxfield School

MY DOG MERCY

I love Mercy, she's the best dog.
She jumps like a kangaroo.
She sits down but only
When she gets food
And she loves me.

Barry Neish (15)
Foxfield School

AS I WALK THROUGH THE PARK

When I go for a walk in the park
I can hear the trees swaying
As the wind blows them side to side.

I can hear the leaves
Crackling beneath my feet
As I walk on top of them.

As I walk past the swings and slides
I can hear the children
Laughing with joy and happiness.

Tammy Lewis (13)
Wallasey School

AN ODYSSEY OF MY FEARS

Prepare for a journey through all of my fears,
A journey of things which I hate,
A journey of things which, when I see them,
Make me scared at a very fast rate.

I hate spiders,
Across the floor,
When they crawl in,
Under the door.

I hate crabs,
From the rockpool,
They scare me,
Just like a ghoul.

I hate jellyfish
From the gloom,
They sting you
To your doom.

You've just heard my odyssey of fears,
A place where hate endures,
I've told you mine,
Now tell me yours . . .

Patrick Pinion (11)
Wallasey School

MY FAVOURITE TIME OF THE YEAR

My favourite time of the year will soon be here.
Tinsel, twinkling lights, festive sounds and my family so dear.
Giving and receiving gifts from one another.
Kissing under the mistletoe, hugging, so glad to be with each other.
The day passes so quickly, seeing people I love with all my heart,
So sad at the end of the day when we have to part.
Watching out of the window, snow falling so fast,
Taking it all in because I know it won't last.
I go to bed so tired from the excitement of the day,
Everything this year has turned out perfect again, what more can I say?

Lisa Andrews (11)
Wallasey School

SPIDER

Spiders moving about,
So quietly,
So quietly,
Spiders moving about.
As I look up, I see a flip chart
and so high up,
It must be the Eiffel Tower.

Spiders moving about,
So gleefully,
So gleefully,
Spiders moving about.
As I look around, I see desks
all around,
It must be the Golden Gate Bridge.

Spiders moving about,
So exhausted,
So exhausted,
Spiders moving about.
As I look up, I see a human
and a so up-straight human,
Agghh! It must be a monster.

Josh Robinson (11)
Wallasey School

SPIDERS ON THE MOVE

Spiders on the move,
So elegant,
So elegant,
Spiders on the move.
Looking at the humans,
They look so lifeless,
Their heads down,
Full on concentration.
Spiders on the move,
So elegant,
So elegant,
Spiders on the move.
It is hot,
I see a clock,
It must be the sun,
I jump on a window,
Thinking it was the way out,
Instead it was an invisible wall.
Spiders on the move,
So elegant,
So elegant,
Spiders on the move.
I'm on the desk,
Dancing about the room,
I made it to the highest ground,
There's a book shooting down my way,
I run . . .
My life has gone,
My spirit has gone,
I have gone.

Simon Watson (11)
Wallasey School

WHAT A GLORIOUS DAY!

It is a tranquil, sunny day,
In the middle of May.
Here I am, sitting on a bunch of hay,
Watching the birds fly away.
Suddenly a refreshing cold breeze,
Whizzes me away,
From the clutches of hay,
Makes me feel relaxed,
And I could not believe it,
But it will never freeze me,
On an appealing, sunny day.

Emma Sloan (13)
Wallasey School

UNREQUITED LOVE

Why do you haunt me like a fox on a scent
Like an eagle on flight waiting to strike its prey?
Leave me alone to console myself
In the horrors of your loathsome face.

What have I done to deserve your undying attention?
Now you begin to terrify me.
Wherever I go I see your hideous face
Looking at me through those grey, lamp-like eyes.

You have done this once before
But it did not last long.
Slowly, very slowly you released
Your menacing hold on my young, innocent soul.

Next you moved on to my also untainted confidante.
Why?
What had she done to obtain your evil glare
Of the desire to overcome her virtuous heart?

And now, back you come to me.
You have almost destroyed me once before
But my steadfast heart enabled me to slowly rebuild myself.

Yet although you have seen the torture you dragged me through
You still come back for more.
Why?

Sarah Perry (13)
Wallasey School

SUNSET BEACH

The soothing waves,
Rippling in caves,
Lapping the shore,
More and more.

The warm, cosy sand,
Feels so grand,
Its golden colour,
Makes the beach look fuller.

Birds swooping by,
From low to high,
Slowly gliding sideways,
Far from all highways.

Rhiannon Lewis (14)
Wallasey School

BOSNIA

The cold winter chill cuts to the bone,
My only warmth is the mist from my breath.
I've no Rockport, LaCoste or Ben Sherman,
In my tattered clothes I stand alone.

My parents they begin to shout,
'Run boy, run. It means your life.'
The men have come, with guns a-swinging,
My mother, my father, tortured no doubt.

I run as fast as my legs will carry, my chest is raw,
A crescendo of orange flames spatter out.
These murderers laugh out loud,
My parents in a heap, on a bloodied floor.

Purumff, purumff, purumff. The silence broken,
The daylight chorus of birds long gone,
Chased away by the demons of war.
From my dream I have awoken.

My heart racing, in a cold sweat,
I've got a PlayStation, bike and happy life.
That great feeling of pure relief,
The children of war, I'll never forget.

Paul Rutherford (13)
Wallasey School

ODE TO PAUL INCE

I was ordering my meal
When my sister came up to me,
And told me there's someone famous.
I asked who,
'Paul Ince' she said.

I got some paper and a pen off my mum,
I went and got his autograph,
He said 'Hi'
I replied with 'Hi.'

He asked 'Who's it to?'
I replied with Hayley.
He wrote on the paper
'To Hayley from Paul Ince'.

That is my poem about
Meeting Paul Ince.

Hayley Cardy (13)
Wallasey School

SEARCHING

I come in search of something
Something precious
Something valuable
Something that means a lot
But although I searched, it was there
All along
Sitting right in front of me
My family.

Rachael Cardy (11)
Wallasey School

FRIENDS (ARE THE BEST)

Some friends are close,
Some friends are gross,
Some friends are happy,
Some are snappy.

All my friends are special,
They're never in my way,
They're always there to help me,
All throughout the day.

Average friends are boring,
Old friends too,
New friends I don't know,
How about you?

Elizabeth Williams (11)
Wallasey School

HOMEWORK

Homework is boring
So is snoring
I get it every day
The teachers get the pay
The kids all moan and cry
'Not homework again tonight!'

Richard Maddox (13)
Wallasey School

ROOM 28

Room 28 is the scariest of all,
Also known as 'Remove'.
The room is so big, which makes me look small,
The door is so tall, if I don't recall.
It makes me scream, the teacher is so mean,
I've never looked in before, they always shut the door.
I'd never like to walk through that door,
I'm telling you I'm sure.

Bradley New (11)
Wallasey School

SCARY NIGHT

Scary night, oh scary night,
What lies beneath that dark sky?
Is it vampires?
Is it monsters?
Is it just the wind?
Well I don't know.
I just jump in my bed,
With my cover on my head,
And drift away in la-la land.

Sam Murphy (12)
Wallasey School

MY CAT

My cat Olly,
Is the cleverest cat I know.
He jumps up and bangs on the letterbox
When he wants to come in.
He opens the cupboard door
And gets his food out,
Goes out of the room and gets someone to follow him
And miaows by the tin.
When he tries to eat the hamster,
Before we can get him
He jumps out of the window and springs for his life.
My cat is the cleverest cat I know.

Alex Murphy (11)
Wallasey School

WALLASEY SCHOOL

Wallasey School is so great,
I just can't get enough.
But when
Teachers shout, teachers scream,
Teachers do the wrong thing.

Teachers polish, teachers gleam,
Teachers always daydream.

Sarah Dean (11)
Wallasey School

NIGHTLIFE

Night
The wind is blowing
The creature scurried to its burrow
Its family, friends
Snuggled on the sofa
Warm as the sun, sitting by the fire.
Summer came they were not seen
Only bones were left
Passing cars and traffic
Pollution killed them all.

Tracy Simmons (11)
Wallasey School

THE JOURNEY

I jumped off the train
finally at the stop.
Standing in the rain
not even a clock.
I didn't know the time
it could be after nine
My feet are killing me
I need a cup of tea.
I asked a stranger the time
he said 'It's two minutes to nine.'
I stood there waiting
waiting, waiting.
But no one showed up
at least not a friend of mine.
Now I am
on the train
all alone, alone, alone.

Natalie McLear (13)
Wallasey School

MY NAN

My nan was old and frail
Her hair a mass of curls
Made up of grey and white swirls.
I close my eyes
And see her in my dreams every night.
She is holding a teddy
With a photo on his chest.
Now I have that teddy
And I feel very blessed.
Nan was very special
She was always there for me.
But now she is gone
And I am very sad.
I feel very empty
But now she is free.

Kathryn Rutter (14)
Wallasey School

RATS

They're very big and smelly
They have a big fat belly.
They have a pink tail
That helps climb rails.
You often find them in sewers
They can be very vicious.
They go up the rusty drain
That comes from the lane.
When they're in the house
You can tell they're not a mouse.

Jessica Harris (11)
Wallasey School

FISHES

F is for soft fins
I is for ice water when winter falls
S is for sharks eating them whole
H is for happiness swirling around their bowl
E is for eating their food
S is for sleeping while they're in the mood!

Charlotte Jones (11)
Wallasey School

The Wind

The wind blows this way
and the wind blows that way
you don't know where it goes
you don't know where it comes from.
Nobody knows.
You don't know when the wind will come
or when the wind has gone
so just be glad that winter
has come at last.

Jemma Hughes (12)
Wallasey School

ALIENS

They came from the depths of outer space,
to perform all tests on us.
They came from the depths of outer space,
on their intergalactic space bus!

They came from the depths of outer space,
they have to come from somewhere.
They came from the depths of outer space,
I wish that they would go back there!

They came from the depths of outer space,
all are nasty and sad.
They came from the depths of outer space,
their names are Mum and Dad!

Gary Philp (13)
Wallasey School

SPIDERS

They run around all crazy,
They're very big and hairy,
They're not at all furry.
You can find them in the hall,
They drive you up the wall.
Some of them are big,
I'm glad they can't dig.
The huge ones are the worst,
If I saw one I would burst.
They really give me the creeps,
A spider I'd never keep.
I hate spiders.

Laura Sturgess (11)
Wallasey School

SPIDERS

Don't like spiders!
All creepy crawly and horrible!
Don't like spiders!
They crawl up slimy drainpipes
And appear in baths.
Don't like spiders!
They have eight horrible, hairy legs
And eyes that gawk at you.
Don't like spiders!
Large ones, small ones,
I don't care.
I hate spiders!

Matthew Edwards (11)
Wallasey School

AT THE RACE

150 motorcross rip around the track
The engines roaring as they race past at 170 miles per hour.
They rip up the track
The crowd cheering as they ride past.
They come off the jumps flying through the air
People all cheering as they come through the finish.
Oh yes, number three is the winner.

Shane Trevitt (110
Wallasey School

MY BROTHER, THE PAIN

My brother is such a pain,
And attention he will gain.
Whenever I'm around he'll give me a pound,
And Mum would come rushing in,
'What's going on?' she said.
'Nothing' said George with a smile.
But of course he was lying,
Because I was crying.
So I ran upstairs and slammed the door.
As you can see, he is such a pain
And there's more to come through the day.

Edward Bayliss (11)
Wallasey School

MY NEW KITTEN

Once I bought a kitten
Which started hissing at my dog.
My dog ran out onto the grass
While inside the house
My kitten had smashed a glass off the window ledge.

It began to get dark outside
Then I heard a bark.
I opened the door
It was my dog shaking on the grass.
I called her in and my kitten saw her
Moved one step forward then fell in the bin.

My mum laughed and pulled him out
Put him in the sink and gave him a wash.
When Mum had finished he looked all posh.
I sat on the couch and looked him in the eye
Then lay him down on my knee
While I drank a cup of tea
Then looked back and he was asleep.

Steven Minshall (11)
Wallasey School

THE SLITHERING SNAKE

Fresh green forest,
Turned to brown, dead leaves,
Only thing in sight is something green
Wrapped around a branch.
Down the tree coming right at me,
It opens its jaw and grabs me,
Down I go onto the floor.
I was rushed to hospital,
Only just recovered.
Every day I went back,
Saw the same old snake,
Until one day I was too late.

Jennifer Bruce (12)
Wallasey School

MY CAR

M y car is small and blue.
Y esterday I went shopping in it.

C reated by Ford it was.
A n excellent Ford Fiesta XR2i turbo injection.
R oar goes the engine as we speed off
   from the traffic lights.

Andrew Johnstone (11)
Wallasey School

DOING THIS POEM

When I was doing this poem
it was a very big disaster.

When I was doing this poem
I ate a lot of pasta.

When I was doing this poem
I began doing it faster.

When I sent the poem off to the
poem makers, I became
a poem master.

Megan O'Neill (11)
Wallasey School

COLD AND WET

Sun, a rainy day
Sounds like thunder
Rain trickling down the windows
It's dark and damp today
Will I be able to play?

Amy Crompton (12)
Wallasey School

FIRST DAY AT SCHOOL

First day at school
Everything is going cool
Walking through the hall
Seeing people playing basketball
Getting new clean books
Meeting new cooks
Being in new classrooms
Looking through my glasses
Now the day is over
A dream has come true
I can't wait till tomorrow.

Debbie Wright (11)
Wallasey School

SECONDARY SCHOOL AT LAST

At last primary school has gone.
Oh no! Reality,
What a long way to go.
I feel quite nervous,
What if I don't like it?
The work is so hard,
Who would have thought it,
It's so big, when will it end?

Football, netball so much to do,
A trip to Tan-y-Graig.
Oh, what joy!
A day away from Mum.
So many friends I am losing count.
It's not so hard,
I think I'll stay anyway!

Aimee Potter (12)
Wallasey School

NIGHTMARE

At night I go to bed
Expecting peaceful dreams
But when I go asleep
I hear screams and shouts

Being chased by monsters
Being chased by rats
Being hurt by zombies
I'm being bitten by bats

I wake up after nightmares
Pains in my head
Hide under my covers
I'm safe in my bed.

Paul Burns (11)
Wallasey School

OCEANS

Oceans can be blue or green,
sometimes they get mad.
Roaring and splashing like
whales in the water.
Large waves crash down really bad.
Oceans can be large and vast
as far as the eyes can see.
Calming ripples swish against the
side of the boat.
The oceans are far too big and
wet for me.

Leigh Farrell (11)
Wallasey School

LONELINESS

Loneliness fills my heart,
Not knowing how I will survive,
Inside, screaming,
Nobody hears,
Nobody cares.

Why was the world defined like this?
No friends,
No real life,
If I had a friend,
Loneliness would fill my heart no more.

Raymond Alan Green (11)
Wallasey School

I'M IN THE SKY

Hi, hi, I'm in the sky
You can see wherever you may be,
I'm floating away
Come and hear me say 'Bye!'

I will float away like a balloon
Heading towards space
For an ultimate prize.

At the end of the race
Before the finish line
You will hear me *pop!*

John Rutherford (12)
Wallasey School

SUMMERTIME

Summer, summer,
Place to be,
For you and me.

Summertime comes
Summertime comes
And summer is a
Place for fun and
You shall come.

Football, football,
Come and play football all day.
Penalty! Penalty!
Free kick, kick it long
Where can it be?

Michael Meek (11)
Wallasey School

THE STARS

Stars, they twinkle up in the sky
Only birds can see them up close
Because they can fly,
While we on the ground
Marvel at the sight.
The birds, they don't care about
Their beauty up there in flight.
As they twinkle in the sky along
With the moon and planets,
We all sit on the ground with the
Earth made partly of granite.

Kelly Burkey (13)
Wallasey School

PAUL AND PHIL

Here is a poem
About my mate Paul
He's little and cute
But not very tall.
He's good at footy
He's fast on his feet
My mate called Paul
Is only three feet.

Here's another verse
About my mate Phil
He's tall and he's lanky
And gets a cheap thrill.
He's a dodgy keeper
For the 'Super White Army'.
My mate called Phil
Is a little bit barmy.

Kat Fernihough (13)
Wallasey School

COLOURS

Orange like the sunset going down,
rocks in Africa falling down.
Yellow like bright daffodils and like the sun's rays.
Blue like the sky on those hot days.
Green like freshly-cut grass, stalks of a flower.
Purple is mystical, magical too, if it has a power.
Will it work for you . . . ?
Red like the colour of vampires' blood,
pretty roses just in bud.
Pink, like love hearts drawn on cards,
Brown is tree trunks sprouting from the ground.
Grey like a dismal night's sky,
the wonder of a Persian cat's eye.
Black like a witch's cape,
        this is the way all the colours *escape!*

Heather Blackwood (13)
Wallasey School

KITTEN

Kitten, running down the stairs
through the hall, under the chairs,
chasing his tail on the floor,
then getting up and running out the door,
climbing the wall, and up a tree
now has got stuck, it's plain to see.
Soon falling down on the ground,
starting to chase his tail around.
Another cat comes to play
but the kitten just runs away,
back in the house, safe and sound,
flopping down to sleep on the ground.

Gemma Poole (13)
Wallasey School

THE STARS

I looked up at the sparkling stars,
they twinkled and flashed in front of my eyes,
I wish I could go right up into space,
and see the planets and all of the stars,
I would love to stand on the moon,
and see the magic and all of the wonders,
the stars shimmer and the planets gleam,
they are so bright, it seems like a dream,
I wish I could go right up into space.

Gemma Sturgess (13)
Wallasey School

MONSTERS

Pale monsters called vampires feed on blood,
Winged lizards called dragons have burning breath,
Twisted humans called warlocks are psychic psychos
With their magic that can't be defeated.
Those purple fiends called orcs wield mighty axes,
Bony corpses called skeletons tend to rise from the grave,
Cloaked skeletons called reapers hold a deadly skull-piercing scythe,
But worst of all, devils are the evilest creatures.

Rob Dean (13)
Wallasey School

DAYDREAM

I look at the space
That lies in front of my eyes
Following the traces of things I can see
My imagination runs wild
As pictures form in my head
I am swept in a sudden daydream!

I see things I like
I see things I hate
Magical and mysterious happenings
In fate and in future
In past and in present
My daydreams are full of hope and desire.

Rachel Stewart (13)
Wallasey School

THE SOUL THIEF

The man with a glass eye,
stared deep into my soul,
He took all my thoughts and feelings,
now he's left a note.
When I go looking,
he's nowhere to be seen,
he pokes and teases me
and he's not very clean.
I'm ashamed and embarrassed,
with no feelings at all,
he belittles me,
and makes me feel small,
I've asked for it back,
but he consistently says 'No.'
I'm feeling alone now,
with nowhere to go.
I realised before that they were not really gone,
I've had them all along.
What I now know is that he
really had none.

Katie McCullough (14)
Wallasey School

HALLOWE'EN NIGHT

Hallowe'en night! Hallowe'en night!
Witches on broomsticks when the moon is bright
They'll bewitch and beguile you
And put you to flight.
Hallowe'en night! Hallowe'en night!

Hallowe'en night! Hallowe'en night!
Vampires are out to give you a bite,
They'll grab you and bite you,
And suck out your life.
Hallowe'en night! Hallowe'en night!

Hallowe'en night! Hallowe'en night!
Ghosts are out to give you a fright.
They'll haunt you and taunt you
And blow out your light.
Hallowe'en night! Hallowe'en night!

Hallowe'en night! Hallowe'en night!
Goblins and gnomes are out for a fight.
They'll punch and they'll kick you,
On Hallowe'en night.
Hallowe'en night! Hallowe'en night!

Hallowe'en night! Hallowe'en night!
All the trick and treaters
Dressed in black, red and white.
And *all* this happens on Hallowe'en night.

Holly Worton (13)
Wallasey School

GLORIOUS FOOD

I looked here, I looked there
There was no more food anywhere.

I walked here and there, still no food
Around I looked, here and there
Still no signs.
I looked up, I looked down,
There it was. It was black and white.

Jamie Saunders (11)
Wallasey School

WHISPERS

As the wind passes through my hair
it whispers quietly, 'Shh, shh!'
If I'm in trouble or I'm feeling down
it whispers, 'Shh, shh, don't cry.'
When no one in the world understands me
I just turn to the wind for help,
as it whispers 'Shh, shh, it's alright.'

I love the wind, it's my best friend.
I like it because it can do me no harm
and when I feel better it still whispers
quietly and softly . . .

'Shh! Shh! Don't cry.'

Kirsty Evans (11)
Wallasey School

THE HEART OF OCEAN, SOUL OF THE BEAR

Whales swinging, swaying on the stormy waves,
Desperate for air but being pushed about by a polar bear.
The bear is roaring and rolling and strolling
It's not going to stop until the shaking thunder shouts 'Halt!'
The ocean will lie still
Like a silky blanket on a sandy shore.
Plop, plop, drop, goes the rain unsettling the blanket
As the whales sing.

Jessica Potts (11)
Wallasey School

MANCHESTER UNITED

Manchester United are the greatest
Andy Cole gets the ball and scores a goal
Liverpool are crap and they are the saddest
Owen gets the ball and falls down a hole
Sir Fergie is the greatest manager
Please! Please! Don't take our Solksjaer away
Roy Keane is the greatest man of danger
I hope the marvellous Beckham will stay
Old Trafford is the theatre of dreams
Sir Matt Busby surely has his own street
Manchester United have sung some themes
Fowler has got a big nose and big feet
Scholes is surely the best midfielder
Sheringham is surely called for England.

Terry Orange (14)
Wallasey School

HOMEWORK

I love to do my homework
It makes me feel so good
I love to do exactly as
My teacher says I should.

I love to do my homework
I never miss a day
I even love the men in white
Who are taking me away.

Vicki Campbell (13)
Wallasey School

THE BIRD POEM

Birds fly so high
Beneath the glowing sky
They fly so high
To touch the sky

But when

Many years go by
To see they touch the sky
Birds go so high
To see they really try.

Nicola Fielding (13)
Wallasey School

DREAM

I am having a dream,
I don't know where I am,
I am dying to wake up,
But I don't know how I can.

I am sitting on a bed,
Something's touching my head,
I hear a newborn baby cry,
I madly wonder why,
I hear the sound of a gun
I see a man run,
The crying has stopped,
The baby is dead,
And I am lying awake in my bed.

Cassandra McMahon (13)
Wallasey School

KILLER

You left me falling forever
I guess you know I hate you
You're so full of sin,
Even the Devil rates you.
Soon, we'll meet
Because I'm coming to get you!

Carl Lewis (13)
Wallasey School

POEM ABOUT ANIMALS

Animals, animals everywhere.
In the sky.
In the sea.
On the land.

Rhinos almost as big as dinos.
Snakes bigger than a garden rake.
Cats bigger than mats.
Animals, animals, everywhere.

Woodlarks almost as big as sharks.
Whales as big as T-rex's tail.
Mice as big as a 5ft pile of rice.
Rats as big as cardboard mats.

Animals, animals, everywhere.
In the sky.
In the sea.
On the land.

Ben Gouldson (13)
Wallasey School

SEASONS

The sun was bright
The beach was hot
The sea was blue.

The leaves were brown
The trees were bare
The air has changed
Autumn's here.

The air is cold
The ground is white
The fires are hot
And Christmas is here.

Winter has gone
And spring is here
Blossom on the trees
Summer is near.

At last, summer has come,
The sun is hot and children run
Another year for the seasons to come
It is worth the wait if you have
Fun!

Vanessa Johnstone (13)
Wallasey School

BIRDS

Swishing, swirling in the sky
Must be the eye of the sky.

Nightingale, lark, blue tit, eagle
Down below a barking beagle.

Swishing, swirling in the sky
Must be the eye of the sky.

Nightingale passes over a skunk,
With some funky spunk.

Swishing, swirling in the sky
Must be the eye of the sky.

Flies in the sky does the lark
Flies until it's really dark.

Swishing, swirling in the sky
Must be the eye of the sky.

Lovely blue is the blue tit,
People down below having a fit.

Swishing, swirling in the sky
Must be the eye of the sky.

Catching prey is the eagle
It really must be illegal.

Chris Wall (11)
Wallasey School

NIGHTMARE

First day at school, no one I know
Silent classroom, oh, will I show?
My heart thumps, my head bangs
Like a drum on its big booming stand.
My body heat rises.
A hiss of sweat on my forehead.
No friendly faces, no beastly bullies.
First day of school, no one I know.
   Oh, will I show?

Suzanne Jackson (12)
Wallasey School

BULLYING

A chip flies across the hall
And lands on the victim's head,
And as food zooms towards her,
She weeps, she cries.

A sudden splatter of ink
And her face is covered,
With oozing blue liquid,
She weeps, she cries.

The threats, the shouts,
The kicks, the punches,
The playground is but a torture chamber
She weeps, she cries.

A mud-ball smacks her in the face
Water soaking one side of her,
Some squashed leaves hitting her chest,
She weeps, she cries.

A poke in her back in the changing rooms,
The whispers quite near her outside,
She hears her name, but it's just a jeer
She weeps, she cries.

No one to tell about the bullies,
Tears shed so many times.
Nobody notices, so she takes a knife,
She weeps, she cries, she's dead.

Hannah Langford Spencer (11)
West Kirby Grammar School For Girls

POEMS

There was an old man from Dundee
Who lived in a hut, in a tree.
He wanted to fly
Way up in the sky
But crashed first flight in the sea.

There was a young girl from Thingwall
Who liked to sing out in the hall.
She sang like a bird,
Without knowing a word,
But broke all the glass on the wall.

Christine Elizabeth Lemon (11)
West Kirby Grammar School For Girls

A Night On A Bare Mountain

Pitch black as a Bible
Wicked witches come to revel,
Flying from the big hole
On their spiky broomsticks.
Dark cats spookily seem to scare,
The creaks and loud cracks from the spirits.

> Ghostly silhouettes climb from their tombs,
> Bony, rattling skeletons,
> White as sheep.
> Assemble to the Devil,
> With his curved horns,
> Red with peril.
> With a trident in his clutches,
> Bright orange pumpkins are lit,

The gruesome ghosts
Party the night away.
Twirling the tango,
Dancing the action-packed night to its conclusion.

> A frenzy of frightening figures,
> Violent vampires,
> Dirty Devils,
> Weird witches,
> Cunning cats,
> Owls hooting,
> Bats swooping,
> More phantoms join the rave.

The rhythmic tune blows out,
As the trumpets blare with joy
And the Devil strikes the strings.

The witches get wilder,
A thrilling event,
Ghostly grins,
Frightening fangs,
Toothless jaws
And empty eye sockets
Stare as the skeletons dance.

An exciting and lively annual event
For the spirits on a Hallowe'en night.
Heart thumping,
Blood racing,
As it reaches a climax.

The time has come to stop the celebrations,
The church clock strikes six.
As the bells chime
Strange, shadowy shapes
Shimmer in the moonlight.

They all wave goodbye with a sorrowful eye
In a sad, sympathetic way.

Daybreak sets
So the spirits go to their Underworld
At the final chime of the clock,
The spirits melt away.

Lisa Jones (11)
West Kirby Grammar School For Girls

I HOPE DREAMS COME TRUE

Bedtime is what I look forward to
Not knowing what dreams will come to you,
Taking hot chocolate in a mug
Drinking it whilst I am cosy and snug.
When the chocolate starts getting sickly
I put on my pjs - really quickly.
I jump into bed and close my eyes shut
I will have a good dream, with a bit of luck.
Now I am floating through the clouds,
All the angels, grouped in crowds.
They all rushed over to greet
Someone I thought I would never meet.
Feeling great, feeling cool.
Am I being a complete fool?
I can't be God, it's only a dream
Though I still remember how great it seemed.
Wishing that I was still there
I know it's impossible, but I don't care.
I love bedtime because of dreams
I love every single fantasy theme.
Now I am ready for another morning
Though I cannot help myself from yawning.
I still can't get over my amazing night
And seeing all that heavenly light.

Gemma Wright (11)
West Kirby Grammar School For Girls

LIFE

Just a little baby, small as can be,
wrapped up in a blanket, sat on mummy's knee.
Drinking from a bottle, sleeping through the day
it was so easy being a baby, fun in every way.

Growing up quickly, to the 'terrible twos'
getting new clothes and brand new shoes.
Crying all the time, eating everything,
but everyone loved us really. I think!

School soon came along, learning all the time,
1-2-3s and a-b-cs - books of every kind.
Children being sick, crying for their mum
If only the end of the school day would eventually come!

Soon we are big teenagers, in moods all the time,
parents yelling at us for every little crime.
Our brains working hard, about to burst!
But forget discos and parties,
Work comes first.

Finding a job, that's what's next,
looking after ourselves, no time for rest!
Cooking our own tea, cleaning our own home,
when is the work going to stop?
I wish I hadn't grown up!

So when you feel fed up with life,
just look at my rhyme.
You are not the only one who is tired and stressed,
All of the time!

Jayne Macdonald (11)
West Kirby Grammar School For Girls

HAPPY HALLOWE'EN

Headless knights and ghastly ghouls,
I love Hallowe'en it really rules!
Trick or treaters knocking at your door,
You frighten them away with an awful *roar!*

Witches and vampires out on the hunt
for sweets and chocolate for their human brunch.
And then they go back to their homes or dens
To stuff their faces with zombies and friends.

Pumpkins and skeletons hung up in the street
with other frightening creatures, you're dreading to meet.
But at 12 o'clock midnight Hallowe'en is done,
that is when the *real* nightmares come!

Charlotte Houghton (11)
West Kirby Grammar School For Girls

SCHOOL'S OUT

The school bell rings
We all run out.
Summer's now here
Get back to the house,
No more school for nearly a month
Time to put the uniform in with all the junk.

No more homework, no more detention,
Now I'm the centre of attention.
All the books go in again, all the toys appear again,
Oh happy day! Come sing! Hooray!
All the kids praise for this day.

Stephanie Noble (11)
West Kirby Grammar School For Girls

THE POEM OF FRIENDSHIP

Friends are kind and always share,
and if you're upset they always care.
If you're feeling sad and down
friends are there to ease your frown.
They make you laugh and are great fun
and play with you, under the sun.
Sometimes we argue but it doesn't last
we put our differences into the past.
We have discos and parties and look really cool,
but we always wear uniforms when we go to school.
We share each others secrets and promise not to tell,
we pass written messages to each other as well.
At the end of school, we have a little play,
before it's time to finish the day.
We go to bed tired and yawning, but happy
that our friends will be there, in the morning.

Rachael Cleator (11)
West Kirby Grammar School For Girls

A FRIEND

Tell me please - what is a friend?
A friend's there for you to the end.
When you're at school, when you're at home,
A friend will wait for you to come.

Tell me more about a friend,
A friend can drive you round the bend.
A friend could be so generous,
Or of course, she could be envious.

A friend could help you on your way
And always listen to what you say.
A friend can help you when times are tough,
A friend will never make things rough.

Okay - now I know what a friend is for,
A friend to open your world's door.
A friend is certainly the best
A friend is better than all the rest.

Emma Fielding (11)
West Kirby Grammar School For Girls

HOPE

I think of hope as being my best friend.
I believe that as well as love, hope is the most important
thing in life.
Where would I be without it?
Well I would be sad!
Knowing for sure that something would come to an end.

Hope is something you can talk to,
Share all your secrets with
And keep tight hold of its hands.

Hope is something you should value
And trust and take care of.

In war, there's always hope that it will come to an end,
There is always the hope that you won't become ill,
Or troubled or scared.

I think of hope as being my best friend,
And so should you!

Jenn Cleave (13)
West Kirby Grammar School For Girls

THE DEEP BLUE SEA

Swimming in the ocean
In the deep blue sea
Speed boats, banana boats
All for us to see
There I spot a dolphin
Swimming with its friends
I splash about, I kick around
The fun never ends
I slip and slither
Flop and flow
In the deep blue ocean
I've yet to know
The wrecks lie deep
Their secrets to keep
Locked on the ocean bed
Waves, they gently lap the shore
While the sand in my toes I happily tread
The water drifts through children's minds
They twist, they glide
Leaving their fears far behind.

Philippa Hirst (11)
West Kirby Grammar School For Girls

A WALK IN AUTUMN

Crisp, crunchy golden leaves,
Blow the wind along the dying hedgerows.
Overhead flocks of birds migrate for winter,
My breath rises before me in the cold morning air.

Dim sunlight shines as the dull autumn sunrise breaks
through the cloudy fog.
A gust of wind tears through the air, making me pull my
scarf far tighter around me.

The moistness in the air turns into rain,
and I race back home.

The warmth of my fire washes over me as though
I've sunk into a hot bath.

I'm here - this is where I want to stay,
at least until spring!

Charlotte Hugman (11)
West Kirby Grammar School For Girls

HAPPY

If I were a seagull
I would glide through the clouds,
And watch the fish swim merrily.
I would swoop down and snatch a fish,
While the waves rocked silently.

The sun would be setting,
The wind would be getting
At the back of my neck.
My eyes would be twitching
For another fish swimming,
So I could snatch it up.

My wings would be moving,
And I would be gliding
High up in the sky.
My fish would be wriggling,
Its scaly skin, fiddling in my mouth.

The waves would be crashing,
While the boats rocked violently.
Foam would be spraying,
The sand would be glistening,
Shells are colourful
In the sunlight.

The sea would calm down,
The boats would rock quietly.
And the seaweed would spread on the sand.
The pebbles would shine
And the sun would come down,
Then silence on the seashore.

Sarah Coral Richards (11)
West Kirby Grammar School For Girls

EGGS, BACON AND BEANS

Eggs, bacon and beans
that's in my dreams.
Carrots, cabbage and green beans
that's in my bad dreams.

If only I could eat burgers every day
that would wash the day away.
If I ate all of my crusts
I think I would turn to dust.

But my mum says 'No!
You cannot go
Until you've eaten your carrot!'
I said 'No! I would rather rot,
than eat a filthy carrot!'

Eggs, bacon and beans
that's in my dreams.
If I ate one more orange
I think I'll go bananas!

Jennifer Evans (11)
West Kirby Grammar School For Girls

THE LONELY MOORS

I wander across the moors,
Everything stays silent and still.
Only me, strolling along
A sea of calm and tranquillity.

Grey clouds tumble across the sky,
Everything seems dead to me.
The purple mountains glowing,
Against gloomy, dark skies.

Though the day is lonely,
I am quite content being by myself.
Just wandering along the water's edge,
My escape route from the cruel world.

The grey skies darken,
Soon day will come to an end.
I start to head back,
Whispering 'I will return again!'

Hayley Fairclough (11)
West Kirby Grammar School For Girls

THE HORSE ON THE HILL

There was a horse upon the hill,
Just looking at the floor.
He looked so sad, just standing there,
I don't think he cared anymore.

That poor horse on the hill.

He was so bony and frail,
Most of his fur had gone.
Then I thought to myself
'Where has this horse come from?'

That poor horse on the hill.

Then one day I saw a man
He said 'This horse is mine.'
I asked 'Why do you neglect this horse?'
He replied 'Just look at him. He's fine!'

That poor horse on the hill.

I phoned the vets,
I phoned them quick
Just looking at that pony
Made me sick.

What is going to happen to
That poor horse on the hill?

The horse was just about to go
When his owner shouted 'Hey!'
But then the vet said sadly,
'That horse is going away.'

That poor horse on the hill.

Then the horse was gone,
He had gone away.
He had gone somewhere nice
Where he could always stay.

That poor horse on the hill.

I was only a child back then,
And now I too, have a pony.
But if I had that poor horse, years ago,
I'd treat him right, if only . . .

That poor horse on the hill.

Sarah Flaherty (12)
West Kirby Grammar School For Girls

RUDOLPH THE BLUE-NOSED REINDEER

Rudolph the blue-nosed reindeer
Wondered why his nose was blue
The other reindeers all had nose-muffs
And he wanted a nose-muff too.

So one foggy Christmas Eve,
Rudolph went to Gran.
'Gran with your nose-muffs so bright
Will you knit me one tonight?'

So Gran got her knitting needles
And then she sat down to knit
When Rudolph came back much later
He found it was a perfect fit.

Rudolph the nose-muffed reindeer
Knew why his nose wasn't blue
The other reindeers all had nose-muffs
And now he had a nose-muff too!

Vikki Johnston (11)
West Kirby Grammar School For Girls

THE SPIRIT OF CHRISTMAS

As winter's cold breath sweeps over the town
It covers the buildings with a white silken gown
Children dressed in mittens with two pairs of socks
Mothers in the kitchen, wearing itchy woollen frocks.

Fathers in their rocking chairs smoking on their pipes,
While the dog sits by the fire,
curling up for the cold winter night.

All the world is quiet, asleep without a care.

As the angels came out of their slumber
to watch over the children there.

Julia Morris (11)
West Kirby Grammar School For Girls

MR WINTER

At night he creeps around the world and sends a sea of mist.
A lake of fog,
A storm of rain,
An evening filled with hail.
He's fierce and bitter when by chance Miss Summer comes to pass.
A sting of wind,
A flash of ice,
A dawn of freezing frost.
And when at night, he creeps around,
A child may chance to see,
His cruel indifference,
As he maims,
The first bold buds of spring.

Rebecca Ryan (12)
West Kirby Grammar School For Girls

HOPE!

When life's the pits and going deeper,
Mountains are high and getting steeper.
Give your hope to the one that you trust,
Feel the joy that someone must
Turn to hope and ask all it's got.
It sorts things out, that you cannot.
It'll have things done, before you know,
Problems done, ready to go.

Look down at the problems that you've just sorted,
Now that they have been deported.
You think of life and all its glory
Spread the word, tell the story.
For now, you've seen the light of hope
You know that you have ways to cope!
Think of hope as your best friend,
It lifts you up at your wits end.
Just think that you now owe it a favour,
Make the most of life and try not to waver.
Go take the rest, have some fun,
Now your problems are sorted, finished, gone!

Libbie Sprigge (12)
West Kirby Grammar School For Girls

MY MUM'S A PIRATE YOU KNOW!

My mum's a pirate you know?
I know it and that's a fact.
For whenever she dices a carrot,
Instead of being cut, it's hacked.

My mum's a pirate you know?
She has a parrot called Polly.
Some of my friends think she's great
Others think she's off her trolley.

My mum's a pirate you know?
With a black patch over one eye.
She has dark brown hair and freckles,
And her eyes are as blue as the sky.

My mum's a pirate you know?
She's sailed the seven seas.
My dad is pretty scared of her
(He shakes and trembles at his knees).

My mum's a pirate you know?
And whether I like it or not
I'll have to get used to the idea,
'Cause this mum's the only one I've got!

Hannah Bradon (11)
West Kirby Grammar School For Girls

HALLOWE'EN NIGHT

Ghosts and ghouls and vampires galore,
all come knocking at my door.
Spells and witchcraft ouija boards too
make me frightened, as white as glue!

Warlocks and werewolves all run amuck
it's enough to frighten the bravest duck.
Zombies and dark lights run through town
everywhere looks an extremely dark brown.

At your door, waiting for sweets
all ready to yell 'Trick or treat!'
Ghosts and ghouls and vampires galore
all come knocking at my door.

Hallowe'en beasts ask for more!

Dorcas Riley (12)
West Kirby Grammar School For Girls

A VERY SPECIAL DAY

There's a very special day on the calendar
A day that everyone should underline
It's a day that's always full of joy and laughter
A day that you could say is only mine.

It happens on October the twenty-ninth
And I do hope the postman knows his way.
It's a secret I have no intention of keeping
Cos if you haven't guessed already
It's my birthday!

Jennifer Harney (11)
West Kirby Grammar School For Girls

HEDGEHOG

Hedgehog coming up the path
Slurping the milk from the old tub bath
Now it's nearly all gone
'Slurp, slurp, slurp!'
Till there's none!
Now he's walking up the path
Leaving behind the old tub bath.
He's also leaving the bowl
Because the milk has all gone!

Jessica Bennett (11)
West Kirby Grammar School For Girls

A DANCER'S LIFE

It's a brilliant feeling up there,
As your feet whistle through the air,
You're travelling fast
Asking 'How long will this last?'

The cold breeze flutters
All you hear is mutters.
All the cheering
All the screaming
The life of a dancer has so much feeling.

Justine McLaughlin (11)
West Kirby Grammar School For Girls

GHOULS AND GHOSTS

Witches with broomsticks
Ghouls in the night
Creep out from shadows
To give you a fright
When ghosts wake to play
There's nowhere to hide
You'd better run now
Because they'll come and they'll bite.

They're coming! They're coming!
Stay under your bed cover,
You're too scared to get up and cuddle your mother!
Witches, devils and ghosts
And believe me, you'll end up as toast!

They're coming, they're coming
Don't even go to the loo.
They're coming, they're coming
Coming to get you!

Helen Louise Wildman (11)
West Kirby Grammar School For Girls

THE UNKNOWN . . .

Swirling, twirling, ever moving on,
Never stopping, don't know where it's gone.
Unknown faces
Far, forgotten places . . .

I used to know where the sun shone,
The darkness came, then it too was gone.
I ran, I fled,
Even I am scared of the dead!

Claire McNally (11)
West Kirby Grammar School For Girls

MY COAST

I stood on the coast, watching seagulls in the sky,
I watch the people and dogs go passing by.
I can hear the waves crashing on the shore,
I don't want to go home any more,
I can smell the salt in the sea,
I can feel the sand tickling me.

I can see the waves go to and fro,
Creatures swimming down below,
Another world beneath the sea,
Another world that is strange to me.
Seaweed, crabs, sand and shells,
Lots of different kinds of smells.

As I climb the rocks and look at the sky,
A swooping seagull passes by,
On the sand, castles I made
With my bucket and my spade.
As the sea swept it all away
I knew that tomorrow comes another day,
To visit the sea, walk on the sand
And hold the seaweed in my hand.

Charlotte Middleton (11)
West Kirby Grammar School For Girls

THE OCEAN

The ocean is rough and wild
Flying fish leaping from wave to wave
The white horses are rushing close
Galloping closer towards the crashing rocks

The ocean is rough and wild
It is an eerie green and brown
Washing up the land
And leaving just a damp and dull world.

The ocean is rough and wild
Swaying from side to side
Swishing and swirling all day and night
From bay to bay.

The ocean is rough and wild
It glimmers in the moonlight
And sparkles in the sunlight
But it fades in the darkness of the night.

The ocean is rough and wild
It travels frantically from ocean to ocean
Through storms and hurricanes
And sunshine and showers.

The ocean is rough and wild
It makes splashing noises
As the waves are crashing together
Fiercely and ferociously.

Robyn MacLaverty (12)
West Kirby Grammar School For Girls

MY FRIEND ALIEN

I went to space one day,
I did not know that I would stay.

My alien friend is not a joke,
But I wish that he would drink Coke.

Lots of people think I am mad,
But I know I am not that bad.

My alien friend likes to play,
He thinks that I should stay.

And I wish with all my might,
That I could go back home tonight.

'Please do not make me stay,
I will do whatever you say.'

'OK then,' the alien said,
'Bring me back your bed.'

And I will set you free,
So you will be as happy as me.

Fiona Shaw (11)
West Kirby Grammar School For Girls

SCHOOL PRISON

The sky is blue,
The sea is too,
The grass is green and lush,
So why am I locked in school
Eating dinner mush?

I wish I could be soaring
Up high with the birds,
But under a strict teacher's nose
I can't say any words.

I wish to be gliding
Around the world so clear,
But . . . I can't do *anything*
Under the teacher's leer.

Secondary school is pretty 'naff',
All work, not any play,
But rest really comes
At the end of the day!

Jamie Burrows (11)
West Kirby Grammar School For Girls

ALIENS

They arrived one day,
In the pouring rain,
Lights flashed in our garden.
I thought it was the police,
But it was worse than that.
I ran to my room,
Grabbed my sister from the computer,
Staggered outside,
Unaware of what was about to happen.
A beam shot out from our big oak tree
And I got a glimpse of what was in the branches.
We ran and ran down the roads,
As if the devil was behind us.
We ran out of town just in time,
We reached the bottom of a hill
And looked back.
A light flashed over the town,
Then everything was *gone!*

Anna Appleton (11)
West Kirby Grammar School For Girls

THE SCHOOL BELL

Five minutes to go,
Come on bell ring,
Oh I just can't wait,
To hear that brring.

Five tiring minutes,
Seems like years,
All the young ones,
Are all in tears.

The stress is too much,
I'm going to explode,
There goes the bell,
We line up, a bus load.

Onto the bus,
Down the aisle,
Onto the seat,
In single file.

The driver's too slow,
I wish he'd go fast,
A few minutes later,
I'm home at last.

Tom, John and Harry,
And of course there's me,
We all play out,
Until it's time for tea.

Helen Foulds (12)
West Kirby Grammar School For Girls

AUTUMN

Icy wind blows and scatters,
Dry leaves and bits of litter.
Twirling, swirling in a spiral dance,
And the squirrels prance,
With conkers in their mouths.

Dappled sunlight on the carpet of leaves.
The wood dispersed with apples, nuts
And autumn flowers.
Birds making nests for the winter,
But there is a splinter,
Of ice on the twigs.

The river is bursting its banks.
Its face is like the sky at sunset.
Strewed everywhere are russet, brown and amber leaves
And the sheaves,
Of corn are cut,
For our harvest tea.

Autumn is a time of bounty.
Food is ever plentiful.
Everyone is feeling kind,
But soon you will find,
Winter is here . . .

Sarah Burdett-Smith (11)
West Kirby Grammar School For Girls

THE ELEMENTS

The first is round,
and not at all flat.
It is pure
and moves with the creatures within it.
This is the Earth.

The second is invisible,
it helps us a lot,
it is thriving,
with other gases,
gliding about the atmosphere.
This is air.

The third is hot,
it has colours of orange,
yellow and red,
it dances in the dark
and flickers in the light.
This is fire.

The fourth is wet,
its bluey-green waves
are as clear as glass,
it swoops and sways
and mops the sandy beaches.
This is water.

Becky Parker (12)
West Kirby Grammar School For Girls

WILD RABBITS

Rabbits hop around all day,
They just love to play,
Sometimes they lay down to rest,
In their tiny burrow nests

They run around everywhere,
But scatter when they get a scare,
People come and gas their homes,
And some small rabbits are left alone.

They dig their homes with a flurry of claws,
And dirty their delicate paws,
Their fur is smooth and soft as silk,
And babies drink their mother's milk.

The bright sun glistens in their eyes,
When they look into the bright blue skies,
The bees buzz around their ears,
And everything around they shall hear.

They love all of the fresh, green grass,
But carrots they can never pass,
Hippity, hoppity, hippity, hop,
The boundless energy will never stop.

Heather Buckley (13)
West Kirby Grammar School For Girls

WEATHER

Rain

Rain on my fingertips dancing everywhere!
Hitting the floor and bouncing in the air.
The soft, wet touch upon my face,
I can remember clearly the sweet embrace.

Sun

Sun in my eyes, finding it hard to see,
Its lovely, warm hands are wrapped around me.
I could in this paradise lie here all day,
Until it decides it's time to go away.

Snow

Its frosty white hands touch my nose,
Brrrr, look it's the colour of that rose.
The ground is laid with a white blanket,
I touched, ouch, it bit.

Wind

The blowing breath blows my hair,
Now it is moving everywhere.
The smell of the sea salt drifting past
And me turning and turning with this wild blast.

Nikita Lewis (12)
West Kirby Grammar School For Girls

A GOLDEN NOTE

A golden note,
A sustaining sound,
A pang of happiness,
A silver strike,
A beauty kiss,
Let it overwhelm you.

A familiar tune,
A nursery rhyme,
An encounter over jazz,
A famous opera,
A slur of notes,
Let it overwhelm you.

A trumpet blows,
An oboe squeaks,
The tuning session's over,
A loud drum roll,
A burst of song,
Let it overwhelm you.

Majestically the notes turn,
Rolling into one another,
Alluring. Refined. Exotic.
Music.

Karolina Griffiths (12)
West Kirby Grammar School For Girls

THAT VERY SPECIAL PERSON

The person who loves and cares for you dearly
The person who makes you see things clearly
The person who tucks you in at night
The person who helps you get over a fright
The person who buys you presents on birthdays
The person who would buy you anything anyway
The person who takes you to school every day
And provides your meals and tidies away
The person who takes you to places real nice
Maybe a concert to see Baby Spice
The person who helps you with your work
And gives you a hug until it hurts
No matter what this person may do
She always will be special to you
The person who will love you till kingdom come
This special person could only be
Mum.

Nicola Kabluczenko (13)
West Kirby Grammar School For Girls

THE GIFTS

I would give as a gift,
The first cry of a newborn baby,
The circle of friendship on Earth,
Peace throughout the world.

I would give as a gift,
The soft, slithery feel of a spider's web,
The scent of a rose in midsummer,
The first faltering steps on a newly born foal,

I would give as a gift,
The sight of a mountain freshly sprinkled with snow,
The smell of fresh pine trees filling the air,
Leaves tumbling to the ground in the autumn breeze.

I would give as a gift,
Thunder and lightning
Striking through the dark night,
The first light at sunrise,
Love from the deepest part of a
Heart kept captured inside.

I would give as a gift,
The smell of the salted seaweed
From the bottom of the dark, deep ocean,
The gasps as fireworks explode into the
Misty night and burst into magical colours,
The sound of the whistling wind.

I will wrap my gifts in,
The velvety starry sky,
Bound with the colours of the rainbow
Sprinkled with the glistening, gleaming, golden sand
From a faraway dessert.

Kim Jones (12)
West Kirby Grammar School For Girls

HALLOWE'EN

Wild witches,
Ghastly ghosts,
Children trick or treating.
Venomous vampires,
Devilish devils
And toffee apple eating.

Face paints, cloaks
And vampire fangs,
A full moon's out tonight.
Witches' brooms and
Wizards' hats,
All pumpkins are alight.

Witches' cackles,
Werewolfs' howls,
Children play duck apple.
Spooky, scary,
Terrifying,
Noises from the chapel.

Trick or treat,
The children say,
Their faces smile with joy.
We give out sweets,
And little treats,
To every girl and boy.

Witches, wolves
And wizards,
Are all what I have seen.
Black cats, rats,
And werewolves,
I love Hallowe'en.

Jo Weldon (12)
West Kirby Grammar School For Girls

THE SONG OF A VEGETABLE

T ime will soon run out for me,
H orrible people will eat me up for tea,
E ating, oh what glorious fun.

S ilver forks and hot cross buns,
O nly the special will not be eaten,
N o pumpkin will ever be beaten,
G lorious peppers on a grand table dine,

O nly with apples and vinegar wine,
F rom the allotment to the table top,

A gony when put in the boiling pot,

V ery appetising I'm sure I will be,
E very minute I think of what will happen to me,
G etting more worried as time goes on,
A s if it is really only a con.
T errible tables with hot gravy pots,
A gony when gravy gets poured on in lots,
B eing a vegetable is no fun,
L iving to know what the day will come.
E very night I think about it lots,
   about being put in boiling pots.

Jennifer Woods (13)
West Kirby Grammar School For Girls

EVACUEES

They traipsed along their journey,
Not knowing what they might meet.
Their hair was full of tangles,
No shoes upon their feet.

No one knew where they came from,
Or who they were,
Their life was a mystery,
To those who did not know.

Their final destination,
They were about to meet,
Shaking like a frightened cat,
They backed into the shadows.

In their lines they stood,
Their hands in their pockets,
Watching people pass them,
Waiting for their name.

They watched their friends go one by one,
There was fear in their eyes,
No one wanted the scrawny lot,
They only wanted the tough ones.

Finally, a lady came,
She took the scrawny lot,
The fear was drawn from their eyes,
As they came out from the shadows.

There they stayed for six whole years,
Through the bad and good,
They dreamed of the day when war was ended,
To them it seemed forever.

Then in 1945 the dreadful war was ended,
They went back to their mother's arms to live their life together.

Louise Parker (12)
West Kirby Grammar School For Girls

MIDNIGHT GARDENS

What was that on the silver lawn?
Shadow apples, glittering bright!
I crept outside onto the moonlit stones
Pulling my gown around me against the
midnight breeze!

Collect a basket from Mum's work store,
Shhh be quiet, don't disturb a thing!
For I think, as the moon is blue,
That my shadow apples are ripe, don't you?

Crouch down small, don't mind the dew,
Pick the apples, one by one
Until your basket's quite full!

See the pixies pick the ripe,
Whisper together, are these the eating type?
Breathe so softly so not to disturb,
Then munch your delicious shadow apples
until the night has gone!

Nicola Hall (11)
West Kirby Grammar School For Girls

HALLOWE'EN

Ghost and ghouls, it's all too scary,
It makes me kind of weary.
At night in the dark I hide in my bed,
While the thought of spooks
Run through my head.

Witches and their terrible laugh,
They never have a bath (pooh!)
Ghosts with their pale white faces,
Haunt you in certain places.

Ghouls with their only red eye,
Focused on you the night is nigh.
Vampires with their terrible fangs,
Is the creature that makes the bangs.

Rebecca Barker (11)
West Kirby Grammar School For Girls

MAGICAL BIRD

An amazing image in the sky
Flashes of silver flying high like a butterfly
An unusual creature
Beautiful colours
A magnificent feature
A huge beak
But it does not sneak
It moves around without a sound
Not falling to the ground
Swoops down nearby
And then up, up it flies
What is it?
It is a magical bird.

Jessica Bryson (11)
West Kirby Grammar School For Girls

THE LIFE OF A REFUGEE

The children sit there, in the black of the night,
Although they have a fire which provides the light.
Their eyes are all weary and full of despair,
The heartless walking past them without a care.
The glowing fire dying, dawn on its way,
The children remain silent, although you hear them pray.

The youngest's eyes so sorrowful, you feel her pity,
But we're strangers to them, as they fled from their city.
Their rags are no good as the white carpet arrives
Miserably they think 'What will become of our lives?'
Suddenly, a miracle - the Good Samaritan returns,
At last the Christmas present which was for what they had yearned!

Yvette Turner (11)
West Kirby Grammar School For Girls

HOMEWORK

Homework is twice as important
But there is always fun
If you get stuck
Always ask your mum!

You need two more paragraphs to finish
But can't think what to write
You just need to concentrate
Then the end will be in sight!

Sara Yang (11)
West Kirby Grammar School For Girls

FRIENDS

F   ab and funky, always fun,
R   eady for an adventure, one on one,
I   n the summer always lively, in the autumn always kind,
      in the winter always friendly, in the spring, always bubbly,
E   ver thinking all about fun, endless ideas, none of them dull,
N   ever arguing, always chatting,
D   ancing around, never stopping, dying down, the fun never does,
S   *pecial friends should be like this one!*

Katie Holden (11)
West Kirby Grammar School For Girls

THE FOUR SEASONS

Spring is the time for new life,
A new beginning for everything.
Every flower peeping through the soil,
But everything will be ending soon . . .

Summer will come with a bright shine,
Glowing, the time for holidays,
Sun, sand and sea with all the pleasures,
But this will be gone when . . .

Autumn will come with a miserable face,
Dull, all leaves falling off trees.
School starts, all children unhappy
But Santa is on his way because . . .

Winter will come white and beautiful,
Presents on their way.
A new year coming and that
Means it is time for a new life for everything . . .

Shams Al-Shakarchi (11)
West Kirby Grammar School For Girls

ESCAPE

Her hair flows down in a long braid,
Not looking back the way she came,
Dirt on the road, dirt in her face,
Hangs her head down in miserable disgrace,
That man wasn't for her, she knew that,
She remembered him clutching her, with claws like a cat,
On her horse, as fast as she can,
Away from the bond with that man,
Her parents should have known he wasn't right,
His cruel face, eyes black as night,
She goes into the distance, galloping home,
Still a girl, still alone.

Eleanor Duncan (11)
West Kirby Grammar School For Girls

WOOD, SEA AND DREAMS

Worms in the wood
Working through
Munching it all
And turning it into dust
Demolishing everything

Waves crashing against the rock
Dulling their senses
Sharpening the edges
To make them like daggers
Deadly and precise
To defend themselves against
The ships of their lives

The dreamer of dreams
Is inside our heads
Conjuring our thoughts
Twisting them to suit
Whatever he wants.

Zoey Cullinan (17)
West Kirby Grammar School For Girls

TO ENVY A SNAIL

A life of simplicity to be envied or not;
In a huge world significance of a dot.
The snail so simple with its house on its back
Its nonchalant life, could we all lack?

A life so free of toil and trouble,
Could even be said 'Lives life in a bubble.'
Slithers through grass, then curls up at night
Hiding away right out of sight.

But is a life like this to be sought after?
A life without joy, love, hope or laughter.
Put in its place, we would probably find;
The life of a snail is not for our kind.

Alexandra R Williams (13)
West Kirby Grammar School For Girls

Hope: War V Peace

There is much anger, much cruelty and distress,
Much hatred and evil,
But little happiness.

I looked all around me and all the time I saw
Destruction, poverty, brutality
And war.

The streets like one big bomb site,
The air all choked with dust,
Tears of homeless children,
This must be stopped, it must.

But how can I make the difference,
What is there that can be done?
Yes, I can do something about it,
I must not let war think it's won.

Kate O'Connell (13)
West Kirby Grammar School For Girls

STREET LIFE

Think about all those children,
Alone on the street,
Very poor and hungry,
With no food to eat.

Lying down in cardboard boxes,
Trying to get some sleep,
Their empty tummies rumbling
And feeling very weak.

I really hope that this will change,
I hope they find a home,
So they don't have to be on the streets,
Crying all alone.

Jenni Shaw (14)
West Kirby Grammar School For Girls

THE DAY HOPE LEFT

I was alone, Hope was gone,
The door was jammed shut,
It would never open again,
As fear started seeping in,
Sweeping over me in a wave of tension,
Would he ever go away?

Quietly, quivering, overwhelming,
Rigid with fright I waited for his next swing,
Allowing the darkness to cloak me,
Wishing Hope would return I remained,
Beating, ranting, raving he would not stop,
Until gradually he retreated into the dark.

Fear was gone but still he taunted me,
How I longed for that door to burst open,
And to see once again Hope's face,
But I only knew Fear now, Hope was gone forever,
My life contained no meaning as I sat alone in that room,
Now no one would help me survive.

How I yearned for Hope to return,
But then a light appeared,
Could it be Hope? I questioned,
As I searched for that feeling of warmth,
I walked to the door knowing she had come for me,
It flew open and she embraced me.

She had come back, my heart skipped a beat,
Light filled the room as my life became complete,
Fear scampered off, he could not fight Hope,
I ran to the door eager to depart,
Fulfilled with joy, my friend had come back
I was safe now, I knew I would survive.

Lindsey Roberts (13)
West Kirby Grammar School For Girls

TRUST

Trust is something always there,
When a friend is near,
Trust is never failing,
Of that I have no fear.

Trust is there in times of danger,
Whether your faith in God or Man,
For whoever you rely on,
Will help you if they can.

It not only applies to humans,
But to animals by the score,
They cannot talk our language,
So rely on us even more.

Not to injure or neglect them,
Which so often is the case,
As humans mistreat animals,
Which degrades our race.

It is important just to know,
There is someone out there you can trust,
Who will help and reassure you,
And rely on them you must.

Faye Coppack (13)
West Kirby Grammar School For Girls

ANGEL'S KISS

I kissed an angel last weekend
And my soul did it mend,
Her lips were like sugar,
As sweet as my mother,
She didn't defend.

I had tea with the devil last night,
His eating habits were an ugly sight,
He scoffed all the beef
And roast meat,
He gave a burp with all his might.

I went to school and Jesus was there,
Dark brown eyes and golden hair,
He gave a wink,
Began to stink,
And he'd done something 'down there'.

I had orange juice with God,
He was almighty and slightly odd,
He sipped and he slurped,
Gave a very gentle burp,
He gave a smile and a little nod.

Lucy Hazlehurst (13)
West Kirby Grammar School For Girls

LENNON'S LAMENT

Help
I've had a *Hard Day's Night*
trying to be a *Paperback Writer*
I'm feelin' kinda low but *Whatever Gets You Through The Night*
is fine by me
I'm lonely so *Love Me Do*
'Cos *I Wanna Hold Your Hand*
so I joined *Sgt Pepper's Lonely Hearts Club Band*
and met a girl called *Michelle.*
now *I Feel Fine*
so we'll walk along *Penny Lane*
run down *Abbey Road*
see *Strawberry Fields Forever*
in a *Yellow Submarine*
but hey I'm just a *Day Tripper*
and I got a *Ticket To Ride*
still we *Imagine*
Instant Karma
and let's *Give Peace A Chance.*
but *Get Back*
these are all *Mind Games*
Lucy In The Sky With Diamonds LSD
I'm trapped in *Cold Turkey*
I'm reaching for the *Revolver*
so *Stand by Me*
but that was *Yesterday* now I say
think love, think life and hey *I am The Walrus.*

Jennifer Stockill (13)
West Kirby Grammar School For Girls

MEMORIES

A never forgotten secret
A horrific memory
All the products of time
Of things that used to be

When the light turned the darkness
All her happy feelings fled
The sadness welled inside her
A wish she'd soon be dead

First to leave was her cheeky smile
The flash of perfect white
Then it was that lively step
Head lowered, she lost her height

Next to go the gloss of her hair
She showed depression with a sigh
Then the greatest loss of all
That glinting in her eye

But I still have the memories
Thoughts that will always be nigh
Of the thing I miss so much
That glinting in her eye.

Jessica Walkup (13)
West Kirby Grammar School For Girls

TRUST HOPE DREAM

I hope there will be peace,
The world, people will trust,
Each and every one - trust, hope, dream.

I wish there could be love,
Agreement, no war, just love,
Each and every one - trust, hope, dream.

I trust there will be faith,
All my friends, my family, faith,
Each and every one - trust, hope, dream.

I feel that I can trust,
My family, the people I love,
Each and every day - trust, hope, dream.

Friends, family, wishes, secrets,
Trust, hope, dream,
Peace emotions, privacy, faces,
Trust, hope, dream.

Hannah Parsons (11)
West Kirby Grammar School For Girls

THE SHOWJUMPER

There was a chestnut showjumper called Pete
Who had dainty, little feet.
He escaped from his stable one day
And ran to the field to play.
All the horses in there challenged him to a dare
And that was the end
Of a chestnut showjumper called Pete
Who had dainty, little feet.

Abigail Looker (12)
West Kirby Grammar School For Girls

My Hamster

I have a little hamster
And it had a broken paw,
I took it on a visit,
A trip to see the vet,
'Goodness gracious, deary me, what have we here?
A fluffy, little hamster,
Let's see what I can do,
A bit of glue and plaster,
I'm sure will do the trick.'
My little hamster's better now,
It's left back paw is fixed,
All thanks to that lovely vet,
My hamster's right as rain,
But I don't think my hamster liked the vets,
Since he won't go back again.

Hannah Lipsey (11)
West Kirby Grammar School For Girls

WHEN

When day and night both mingle,
And dusk cloaks all the world,
Nothing breaks the silence,
As it echoes, unheard.

When time begins to follow,
The future in its path,
Nothing dares to follow,
As daylight turns its back.

As black as any night could be,
As drowned as any sorrow,
Nothing comes and nothing goes,
When new hope fills tomorrow.

Rebecca Sullivan (12)
West Kirby Grammar School For Girls

GHOSTS

Ghosts can be friendly, nasty or mean,
No matter what, they can never be seen.
Some like to hide then shout 'Boo!'
Others go 'Ah, ah, achoo!'

Baby ghosts like to rattle stuff,
But then their mummy tells them off.

Ghosts like to scare people in the night,
Better watch out cause they'll give you a fright.
They creep around the house tiptoeing quietly,
Hidden in the shadows where no one can see.

Anna Poldervaart (11)
West Kirby Grammar School For Girls

HOPE AND TRUST

I hope to be a vet
helping all those animals in need
I hope to be a doctor
and cure patients who bleed.

I trust many people indeed
my mum, dad, nan and gran
I love them all very much
I love them as much as I can

I hope to be an archaeologist
and dig all those rocks
I hope to be a clock maker
and fix a lot of clocks

I trust my pets
apart from the bird
She bites and nips
and I can't think of another word.

Francesca Irvin (11)
West Kirby Grammar School For Girls

A THOUSAND GRAINS OF SALT

A thousand grains of salt
I tip onto my fish and chips
I eat it carefully
As it passes through my lips.

A thousand grains of salt
All over the kitchen floor
I swept it up with a brush
So it's there no more.

A thousand grains of salt
In the sea water on the end of my spade
I poured it onto my sandcastle
Which my brother and I had made.

A thousand grains of salt
In the Marmite I spread on my toast
Melted butter and Marmite
Is the thing I like the most.

Rachael Fear (11)
West Kirby Grammar School For Girls

HOPE

Hope,
A bright, sunny yellow,
Hope is what keeps us going,
Through the twisting road of life.

Hope is a longing,
Sometimes to be happy,
Sometimes for love.

Hope can be for good looks,
Or to be rich.
It is a kind of wishing,
A sort of fantastic dream.

Hope,
A bright, sunny yellow,
Hope is what keeps us going,
through the twisting road of life.

Frances Harwood (11)
West Kirby Grammar School For Girls

MOONLIGHT

It lights up the sky
like a lighthouse
showing sailors
the way home.

A couple walking hand-in-hand
on a dusty shore
as the night gets older
the moonlight gets stranger.

At night I think of my heart's desire
I sit upon my window sill
I start to shiver as I look at the moonlight
get captured in a daze
by the prince of dreams.

Kyrie-Anne Grainger (12)
West Kirby Grammar School For Girls

HOPE

Hope is an ongoing feeling
It is a desire from inside
A light at the end of the tunnel
That brings a new wish to our lives

The key to it is don't give up
And keep being optimistic
Something you can work for each day
A new toy, new bracelet, new ring

Some people go through horrid things
Things like desperate poverty
They always put their children first
They need a new hope, a new dream

All they need is a brand new hope
An incentive to keep going on
One day they will have what they want
Something they will be proud of.

Kari Miles (11)
West Kirby Grammar School For Girls

MY WISH

For Vie Mannsell

This is my wish - to see my relatives,
especially my granny.
This is my wish - to choose my favourite colours,
like a rainbow of my choice.
This is my wish - to have a gift of drawing
pictures of paradise.
This is my wish - to trust a friend who will say
'I will ease your mind.'
This is my wish - to say hello to everyone
who will read *my wish*.

Jennifer L Turner (11)
West Kirby Grammar School For Girls

THE RUINED MANOR HOUSE

All alone
Desolate
In the windswept moors of Wales
Fir forests to the right
Farms to the left
It is there when the sun shines
Holiday makers clogging up the roads
It is there when the mist forms
Covering up bits of stone
Gargoyles and broken, mossy balusters
It is there when the rain falls
Making puddles in broken flagstones
When the snow falls it is there
Turning the green grass into a white carpet
Sheep graze now
In the great panelled hall
Munching the grass
Where noblemen once ate
But when the sheep are dead
The manor lives on
A remnant of a long-forgotten era
Yet
Though it has long been utterly ruined
It's still lived in
Sheep, starlings, crows
Nestle in alcoves, nooks and crannies
Underneath the fire place
It has grown old gracefully
Becoming beautiful in its old age
Nature's reclaim.

Adrian Pascu (12)
Wirral Boys' Grammar School

THE STORM

As the clouds begin to cover,
Rain starts to batter.
The wind picks up speed,
And lightning starts to strike.
I watch all this as it happens,
And I let the storm take its turn.

Nick Page (12)
Wirral Boys' Grammar School

THE SAVANNAHS OF AFRICA

Over the blue hills rises a flaming orb,
Reflected in every dewdrop
And pumping life into the surrounding knot,
The animals are awake and audible.

Down by the lake the animals drink,
Each mouthful appreciated and used well,
In a faraway tree is the screech of a bird,
The dewdrops are gone but where?
This place is enchanted.

Sam Thistleton (11)
Wirral Boys' Grammar School

DARK CRATER

Clouds of billowing smog
Acid falls as rain
The rumble of machines
The whirr of cranes
The world is a pit
Full of manmade pain
For the forests and the rivers
Because the world is becoming a . . .
Dark crater.

Jason Barton (11)
Wirral Boys' Grammar School

RUGBY

Raging rugby all rugged and rough,
Tigerish team mates all tattered and torn,
Fast and flowing with fleet of foot,
Tight and tense, terrific and tough.

Muddied marauders, messing and mauling,
Blistering bodies all battered and bruised,
Silly spectators shouting and screaming,
Captains courageous all cunning and calling.

Pacy performers, passing and punting,
Fiercesome forwards, fighting and foraging,
Dirty days always dreary and dull,
Horrible 'Harrys', hounding and hunting.

Chris Beckett (11)
Wirral Boys' Grammar School

SAILING

Her sails billowing full with wind,
Her hull cutting through the waves,
She sails the Atlantic blue,
Throwing herself against the wind,
Frightened of the watery depths.

The dark creeps in, the silence comes,
The wind whips up and the waves they grow,
Suddenly the rocks loom near,
But the ship is gone, crashed on rocks,
Beneath the water, beneath the rocks.

Andrew Mackenzie (11)
Wirral Boys' Grammar School

THE SUDDEN CHANGE

The heat of the sun is burning me, but a cool breeze
makes me shiver.
The bright reflections off the sea dazzle me.
The faint smell of the salt from the ocean leaves a bitter
taste in my mouth.
And the calm sounds of the ocean waves scaling the
shore soothe me.

A dark shadow casts over me like night's cloak.
The temperature rises up and up.
The sea hisses and bubbles to boiling soup of filth.
I choke on the strong smell of acrid decay.
Explosions send glowing fireballs that fall to the
ground like cruel fireworks.
Clouds of ash cover me.
The ground is now dirty orange and black like old confetti.

Jonathan Green (12)
Wirral Boys' Grammar School

Paradise

As I sit upon the rocky shore,
The gentle sea lapping at my feet,
I breathe in deeply and smell the scent of daffodils in bloom.
The idle chattering of the birds fills a still sky,
My eyes are dazzled by the brilliant light,
Casting long, black shadows across the coast.
In the smooth, azure sky a wispy streak of cloud gracefully
drifts across the horizon,
A docile breeze warmly caresses my skin,
I close my eyes and slip into contented slumber.

I wake,
And never has the sound of silence been so painful to my ears.
A mass of rubble still pours down the hillside,
Scarring the landscape for an eternity,
The smoke rising from the carnage makes me cough and choke.
A sole tree survives,
Its bark is black and disfigured,
Its trunk is bent over like an old man's back.
I hear the faint cry of the earth calling for me to relieve its suffering,
Again I fall asleep but not to awake.

Peter Baxter (12)
Wirral Boys' Grammar School

THE STORM

A deepening growl,
A deathly black ripple of cloud,
A sharp wind, breathing faster and faster
A whirr, a mumble, a roar, a crack
A great crackle and an almighty jolt,
A rustle and a whoosh and an ear-splitting crash,
A torrent of battering water plummets from above,
The aggressive black, pouring in sheets,
A frequent gale, a sudden flash, a ricocheted boom
A snappy, whoosh, a jolt and a bang,
Quickly followed by a large slash,
A swoosh and a crash, a bash and a slam,
A thud, a clatter and a mind-numbing pain,
A tree is a flame, with a whirl and a whoosh,
A plip and a plop, a splash and a groan,
A fire is started; a fire is out,
A tear trickles down the sky,
A deathly black ripple of cloud,
A deepening growl,
The storm,
Has passed.

Scott Anthony Martin (12)
Wirral Boys' Grammar School

AUTUMN

I am wearing marigold and crimson in shapes of leaves.
I hate winter, it is the breath of a mortal enemy.
I hate spring for its gentleness, the people walking in shorts
and T-shirts.
I am the mightiest of seasons - autumn.
My hat is as black and dark as the fur on the panther.
My cloak of burnt ash and crimson leaves.
I suspiciously move, my roar is like rockets
as I blow on the people.
I love the summer, as I can show my power.
Huff, puff, I will blow a cloud over it.
Ha! Ha! Ha!
I am champion of the seasons.

Hao Win Li (11)
Wirral Boys' Grammar School

A WOLF'S FEAST

My silver coat shines like a crown,
eyes locked on that deer so brown.
In the freezing cold weather,
with the ground full of heather.

Ready to pounce,
adrenaline pumping through every ounce.
One, two, three,
'Deer, come to me.'
In the freezing cold weather,
with the ground full of heather.

I'll take her home to my mate,
our food is a deer's fate.
Through the shimmering snow,
dragging along the captured doe.
In the freezing cold weather,
with the ground full of heather.

Here in the forest all must learn
if they ever want to return,
that I am the king
and these animals just servants.
In this freezing cold weather,
with the ground full of heather.

Michael Newland (13)
Wirral Boys' Grammar School

ENVIRONMENT

I breathed the air, pure, clean and fresh,
I gazed upon the grass so green and lush,
I smelt the fresh morning dawning,
Dew and pollen forming tiny droplets
Like tears upon the bush.

How wonderful the earth can be,
When nature is left alone.
No pollution and smoke, rubbish and mess,
Dumped by humans creating trash.

Cars galore causing fumes and smog,
No thoughts for friends or foe,
Only concerns are for speed and ease,
No care for the natural world.

Ben Whitehead (12)
Wirral Boys' Grammar School

AN AUTUMN WALK

An autumn day can often be
So beautiful, so blustery
To take a walk on such a day
Is a wonderful experience.

To wander down a narrow lane
With wild blackberries here and there
With birds that sing whilst in their nests
And flutter with their tiny wings.

To cross over a wooden stile
And jump into a grassy meadow
To see and smell the freshly cut grass
And listen to the blackbird's song.

To walk along next to a field
With cows looking up in surprise at you
And other cows who eat so steadily
Whilst you pass by, barely noticed.

To carry on and up a hill
With a fabulous view at the top
To rest awhile with aching limbs
And catch your breath in wonder.

As you come down, interrupting rabbits
That play peacefully, oblivious to danger
They stop and look at you surprised
Before scampering back to their burrows.

You head for home, passing through a wood
Feeling dark and strangely mysterious
You crunch upon the golden leaves
And see the squirrels collecting nuts.

You round a corner and see your house
And feel almost disappointed
But, to have seen the country in its full splendour
Is truly a wonderful experience.

Ian Mahers (12)
Wirral Boys' Grammar School

THE SNAKE

The snake is a clever creature,
Sly, cunning and wise.
His long, twisting coils, a distinctive feature,
That wrap around his prize.

Under the canopy, he keeps himself awake,
He does not chase his prey,
Because he is far too smart,
Instead, he eats when they come his way.

He slithers round his victim
And waits for the time to squeeze.
His victim doesn't know it yet,
But he is about to freeze!

As now the time has come
To give his victim a fatal hug
And to devour his lifeless prey whole,
Like swatting an insignificant bug!

Stuart Murray (11)
Wirral Boys' Grammar School

THE STORM

It was a dark, dark night,
Suddenly it was not.
A white flash of lightning,
Spread across the black sky.

Fingers stretched forever,
My eyes followed their trail
Until they disappeared,
Everything was silent.

It seemed like hours and hours
As I stared at the sky.
Then an almighty crash,
The storm filled me with fear.

One great roar of thunder,
Followed by another,
I was standing so still
As the storm raged above.

Tom Richardson (11)
Wirral Boys' Grammar School

THE GREAT BIRD

I can see a bird in the sky,
It sparkles in the sunlight.
It swoops swiftly down towards me.
Sitting down on a rock, I stroke it.
Its claws are clenched; I stroke it again,
Its golden eyes staring at me.
I had made a wonderful friend,
I think he had made one too.

Being with the bird felt like ages,
Its great golden eyes still fixed on me.
Its bright blue wings, sparkling,
Among the rest of his feathers.
He walks even closer to me,
Jumps up and sits perched on my arm.
We say goodbye to each other,
He leaps off my arm and flies away.

James Meyerowitz (11)
Wirral Boys' Grammar School

SPACE

Five minutes to go, the countdown had started.
Sweat fell from my face, onto the control panel.
Three minutes to go, I was feeling scared.
One minute left, boosters engaged, engines fuelled.
I closed my eyes tightly and started to pray.
Thirty seconds to go, we powered up the systems.
Engaged all engines, we had lift off.
Travelling through space at the speed of light.
Our journey into the unknown had just begun.

As I looked around the dim blackness of space.
I marvelled at the emptiness before me.
We raced towards Mars. It shimmered with reddish light.
We boldly went where no man had gone before.
We sought new life and discovered new planets,
Wishing to encounter new civilisations.
Our mission was always to go in peace.
But who knows what the blackness hid from us?

Nicholas Wood (11)
Wirral Boys' Grammar School

THE BEAST

As I lay in my bed
Trying to get some sleep
A thought kept going through my head
I was thinking shall I have a peep

I open my bedside drawer
To get my chocolate feast
Then a knock came on the door
Was it a chocolate-eating beast?

I let out a yell and a shout
As she came into my room
I cried get out, get out!
But I had a feeling of doom

As she walked closer to my bed
I saw there was no need to bother
Because she had already been fed
In any case it was only my mother

Carl Scarisbrick (11)
Wirral Boys' Grammar School

SPACE TRAVEL 1969

Space the final frontier.
The fiery engines roaring
Blasting off into the great unknown,
Hope of explorations on their calm minds.

Shooting out of this world,
Going where no man had gone.
Fascination on the great landing,
The very first step on a new planet

The famous flag planting,
The eyes of the world watching,
The memorable *'first step for man'* speech.
The fabulous splash on the returning.

The welcoming of space heroes,
The entire world congratulating
A time to celebrate everywhere again,
The famous moment remembered forever.

Benedict Smith (11)
Wirral Boys' Grammar School

WAR

How the hell did it all begin,
The noise, the smell, the fear and the pain,
No-man's-land, we must all be insane,
Conjuring up the guts to stick it in,
Then telling yourself it's not a sin,
No man's land, what an appropriate name,
Everyone here is going insane,
Despite the cost we've got to win.

Mutilated bodies, tears frozen in place,
Agonising screams of pain and fear,
Penetrate through the most hardened ear,
What's happened to the human race?
No man's land? No man's gain,
Everyone here was insane.

Michael Procter (13)
Wirral Boys' Grammar School

NO NAZIS IN BRADFORD

Two children stand alone in town
One is tiny the other tall
And written on a nearby wall
'No Nazis in Bradford'.

Thinking of times gone by
Without a tear or a sigh
The two of them know why
'No Nazis in Bradford.'

Thinking of what they used to have
Thinking of those they used to love
Thinking of their once easy life
No troubles, no strife.

All because of one man's madness
They stand alone now
Filled with sadness
'No Nazis in Bradford'.

Kevin Garvey (13)
Wirral Boys' Grammar School

RULER OF THE NIGHT SKIES

The majestic white owl
Spreading its plumage in animal glory
The wings extended like angels'
A bird not to be tried

The majestic white owl
The piercing eyes, their stony glare
They show no fear
They have no fear

The majestic white owl
The mouse hanging from its bloody beak
Lifeless, killed with a swipe
Its pathetic limp body: insignificant

The majestic white owl
Ruler of the night skies
Controlling the rhythm of the night
Adding its own beats
The majestic white owl

James Swinburne (14)
Wirral Boys' Grammar School

WHO AM I?

Who am I anyway?
Sitting in this doorway
Thinking of the past
The good times, before the drugs

Who am I anyway?
With nowhere to go
Sitting all alone,
Waiting for something.

Who am I anyway?
With no family,
All of them gone,
All because of me.

Who am I anyway?
An insignificant social outcast,
Nothing left in life,
Nothing but to die.

Who am I anyway?
Sitting all alone
With no one to love me
And no one to hold.

Who am I anyway?
There's nothing left for me,
I sit in my doorway and think -
Who am I anyway?

Michael Tasak (14)
Wirral Boys' Grammar School

THE MATADOR

When the big night comes,
It's time for the fight,
I pick up my red cape,
And focus my mind.
I have to think straight,
Not let my mind wander;
I have to hold my fear
And concentrate hard,
But all I can think of
Is that bull's evil eyes.
They stare right at me,
Deep into my mind.
It knows all my fear
That I cannot hide.
I feel its eyes burn;
They can see into my soul.
I know the time has come;
The bull lies in wait.
It knows my time has come,
And what will be will be.

David Smith (14)
Wirral Boys' Grammar School

FIRST SNOW, FIRST HURT

A solitary figure huddles on a street corner,
Dressed in lace barely protected by a skimpy jacket,
Crystals like tears glitter upon her ears,
                    her face streaked with black.

Her fingers numbed by the fierce wind that cocoons her,
She battles her way back alone, alone,
Guided by the grainy moonlight.

First snow, first hurt.
Unforgiving pain runs rife.

As winter offers its hand to the world,
The girl repairs her broken heart with memories of her love.

Michael David Wood (14)
Wirral Boys' Grammar School